The Color of Winter

poems by

Eve Forti

Finishing Line Press
Georgetown, Kentucky

The Color of Winter

Copyright © 2018 by Eve Forti
ISBN 978-1-63534-811-8 First Edition
All rights reserved under International and Pan-American Copyright Conventions.
No part of this book may be reproduced in any manner whatsoever without written permission from the publisher, except in the case of brief quotations embodied in critical articles and reviews.

ACKNOWLEDGMENTS

I am grateful to the editors who first published these poems, sometimes under different titles and in earlier versions:

Goose River Anthology: "Thanksgiving"
The Pegasus Review: "Tomorrow"
Veterans for Peace Journal: "A Dream Meeting With Anne Frank"

Publisher: Leah Maines
Editor: Christen Kincaid
Cover Art: Suzanne Forti
Author Photo: Maria Burnham
Cover Design: Eve Forti

Printed in the USA on acid-free paper.
Order online: www.finishinglinepress.com
               also available on amazon.com

Author inquiries and mail orders:
Finishing Line Press
P. O. Box 1626
Georgetown, Kentucky 40324
U. S. A.

Table of Contents

The Color of Winter 1
Dressed for Trouble 2
The House with a Veranda 3
Catechism Lesson 4
That October 5
Thanksgiving 6
Come December 7
Wings 8
Promised Land—1908 9
One Night with Pablo 10
Argentina 11
The Rapture of Bernini 12
Then Julia Read 13
Reluctant Archeologist 14
Night 15
Tables for Ladies 16
What News on the Rialto? 17
The Doppler Effect 18
Blues 19
A Wintry Tale 20
First Snow 22
Stars 23
A Dream Meeting with Anne Frank 24
Tomorrow 25
Life Lived 26

"The Heart Is Forever Inexperienced."

~ Henry David Thoreau

THE COLOR OF WINTER

I am never ready for winter's icy ravages
    the absence of light

I prefer to dream of spring
    the lilac bush lush with color
        outside my front door every June

and yet the color is not truly lilac
    it is a dark purple-blue

the color of long January nights
    of thin ice on a deep pond
        of blood thickening in the veins

DRESSED FOR TROUBLE

In the old family album
a little girl dressed up
as if for Halloween

in one photo wearing
a badge
and her grandfather's police hat

in another sporting a hunting cap
wading boots and a pipe
leaning on a rifle

there she is again dressed for trouble
this time
in an army jacket and officer's cap

no doubt in preparation for battles
recorded and not
that would come again and again

THE HOUSE WITH A VERANDA

The house where I spent
much of my early childhood
in a basement flat
is no longer there
torn down
bulldozed
disappeared

now only a small rocky space
remains
without trees or flowers
or any sign
that a house once stood there

no path to or from that long ago
nothing to remember or forget

CATECHISM LESSON

The war was finally over,
but forty-eight first graders
were still interned.
Our warden carried a wooden ruler
and we were scared
within an inch of our lives.

Sister taught us the Act of Contrition
and made us believe we needed it.

Confined too
in a floor-length black wool habit
chained with gumball-sized rosary beads,
her face bulged crimson
wimpled in starched linen.

Fidgety, breathless,
we listened for our names
that last day of school.
If unacknowledged
it meant another year with her.
As forty-one of us stood shivering
against blackboards and locked windows,
seven sat sobbing at their desks.

We learned more that year
than Sister ever thought she taught us.

THAT OCTOBER—1962

Young maples crowded their quarter acre
foliage quaking
dying red
outside a windowless cellar where she huddled
with two toddlers and a portable radio
tuned to Armageddon

as crisis mushroomed
she longed to run free
to break limbs off trees
to pile crisp leaves
stockpile mulch for her seedlings

a hasty defense against a new kind of winter
scant provision
for a year that might not spring

THANKSGIVING

Glassy-eyed, gutted,
they hang
from a neighbor's maple tree
where months earlier
sweet syrup ran
and weeks earlier
a child's green swing
rocked in a sudden breeze.

In autumn deer provide
a feast for him and food
for thought reminding me
of cycles and struggles,
how quickly things can change.
Reminding me
I'm far from spring,
still hungry for life.

COME DECEMBER

No fear, drear, or dread.
No thoughts of sticks or chairs.
My young grandson
(that ingenious architect
of imaginary buildings)
plans to put wheels on my sneakers
then whirl me around
to wherever I want to go.
We will dance in circles
or squares to our own music.
Have fun.
Something to look forward to
when autumn is gone.

WINGS

Beyond lobster boats
and brightly colored buoys

above islands
carved away
by ancient ice

wild geese soar
from northern breeding grounds
to someplace warm

wings flapping
like so many linen
handkerchiefs

like fine ladies waving
au revoir
at the start of a long ocean voyage

PROMISED LAND—1908

Her full hips hid beneath billows
of smoky wool

her eyes as dark as Etna's ash
searched open sea and sky

photos and mementos torn from yesterday
cut into her clenched fists

she wanted to be half-way
before flinging them overboard

before drowning her old self
in an ocean of forgetting

before her rebirth in the New World
Columbus had discovered for her

ONE NIGHT WITH PABLO

Watching *Il Postino* for the umpteenth time
I sat restrained squinting at the captions
until the raspy music rubbed my ears
and he pressed himself against her

that perfect tango brought me to my feet
in search of a Neruda poem
to sweep me in a light fantastic way
away from there to anywhere overgrown
with bougainvillea
or that overlooked the Adriatic

one freeze-framed night of untranslated poetry

ARGENTINA

In my dreams
I learn to dance the tango

take long strides
between long pauses
move in 4/4 time

I pause somewhere
between the Andes and Atlantic
usually in Buenos Aires

the music haunts my soul

in my waking hours
I will never dance the tango
or ever go to Argentina

but I may lie down some bright day
on freshly fallen snow
and pretend my arms are angel wings

pause and flutter soundlessly
somewhere between the Appalachians and Atlantic
in my existent world of dreams and cold

THE RAPTURE OF BERNINI
Ecstasy of St. Teresa in marble
Gian Lorenzo Bernini   1598-1680

How could he have known what ecstasy looks like?

Fixing her between passion and pain
Beatitude and gravity
Between Heaven and Earth

How did he make the marble cooperate?
Chipping away the paradox
Carving cold stone into white heat
Of heavenly bliss even angels cannot know

How could he have known?

THEN JULIA READ

Buttoned to boredom, dozing
with one eye shut to moons,
Junes and spoony rhymes,
I stirred to a voice
threading pearls, puckering
the silk of my half-dreams
by reading his words
as if they were her own.

I cannot imagine Rilke being read
with more passion
except maybe by a woman he had loved.

RELUCTANT ARCHEOLOGIST

Tapping my foot against worn rungs
on my old desk
listening to Vivaldi's *Le Quattro Stagioni*
over and over again
I imagine the joy of hearing
his music for the first time
maybe in a gondola on the Grand Canal
maybe at sunset   maybe in September

there's a Hunter's Moon tonight
I wonder what you're doing now
if you remember   if you've changed
if you're still breathing
I know no grave   no etched granite
but you're entombed
exactly where I've forgotten
the heart's a complicated place
and I'm afraid to dig

NIGHT

Before the words
before the bang
before light brushed glare
on everything
was endless night

I love the night

when mirrors are inoperative
allure takes on new meaning

freed from frivolous assessment
we beckon beauty from within
scent   sound   touch

I love the night
your smell   your voice
to reach for you in darkness

TABLES FOR LADIES
    Edward Hopper, 1882-1967
    oil on canvas, 1930

The room is rich
and ripe
rife with walnut paneling
and fruit
the white where it is
is very white
chip-crisp
pure

whereas the conga line
of perfect yellow
grapefruits
and basket filled
with things tropical
make me hungry
for palmed islands
and wild dates

WHAT NEWS ON THE RIALTO?

We toasted your mysterious life

Postcards from everywhere
Photos of you two-dimensional
Against the Great Wall
The Sphinx and pyramids
The Bridge of Sighs

Some say you ran with the bulls
And climbed the Matterhorn

Could be
I will never know
But I do know I like to pretend
You were Double-O-Something
Not just some weary globe-trotter

With a house full of souvenirs
And a filled-in passport

THE DOPPLER EFFECT

The speed of stars
and the end of love
are gauged the same

a change in frequency
of energy waves
when bodies are moving apart

as galaxies spiral out of view
and distant suns grow red
in their rush away from Earth

there is one last burst
of energy
that sears their hearts

her cheeks flush
as his words slide into a black hole
they have discovered in their heaven

meteors
Saint Lawrence's tears
stream from the constellation Perseus

as waves of shifting light
drown hope after hope
dream after dream

and preparing to be strangers
they drift apart
a universe expanding between them

BLUES

Earth is blue
a whirling swirl of sea and sky
but sorrow is bluer

bluer than hot stars in the center of the Milky Way
bluer than the gas planet Neptune
bluer than seas
an illusion
clear not blue except from above

bluer than the giant star Mimosa
bluer than the thirteenth full moon of the year
bluer than sky
an illusion
clear not blue except from below

Earth is blue
but sorrow is bluer
not clear except from within

A WINTRY TALE

The Beginning

From out of nowhere it comes   a bite of a spider in the night
a snake hidden in a pile of leaves grabbing at an ankle or calf
a lightning bolt on a sunny day
somehow you have fallen onto the *third rail* of pain
suddenly you are in its grip with no end in sight
            no remediation
nothing but the clock and calendar to remind you
that your life has changed   maybe forever

The Loneliness

Pain is a jealous lover   wanting you all to itself
not letting you think about anything or anyone else
            all consuming
it is difficult to comprehend the loss and loneliness
trying to remember who you were before the pain
before you became *that person*
the one other people feel sorry for but cannot understand
when asked how you are they want to hear you say
"Fine…just fine…thank you"

Others

You can not guess or judge another's pain
like fingerprints pain is individual   *one of a kind*
there is no pain meter or threshold measurement
            no one size fits all
if someone tells you they are hurting
believe them

How It Feels

In Luke's Gospel it tells how persistent prayer works
knock on a friend's door even late at night
and he will finally come down
to give you what you ask   what you need
you have broken down the door and smashed the windows
            with *prayer*
but the house seems deserted   as if your friend has moved away
and left no forwarding address

Help

You say that you do not want to be a bother
to be *needy*   to ask for help from friends or family
I say you are doing them a favor…asking
allowing them to escape their own lives
            for a short while
letting them into your world
to drive you   feed you   help you
it is a gift you give to them
it is good for the soul

FIRST SNOW

Summer's promises
hide shrouded
under mounds of white
no wither seen

just fence and bench
frosted urns and scattered dots
of yews and twigs

until the melt
when
hibernating hopes awake
and winter's gray
construction paper sky recedes

when
tulips rule the scene
in every shade
and icy recollections fade

STARS

It's snowing stars
all drift and glitter
blinding
in the early morning light

let's get a sled and shovel
move a bit of heaven
and then glide through it

A DREAM MEETING WITH ANNE FRANK

The café was dim. The time was dream.
She fingered the lace tablecloth
as if it were the bridal veil she never wore.
As she raised her dark eyes I asked if she said it.
She smiled and gazed down again.

I saw a child in the face the world can't forget.
Eras now flown, yet she's still only fifteen.
Alive in the hearts of us doomed to remember.
She glanced at my watch. Time was precious
and fleeting. I grasped at her hand to keep her
from fleeing, though I knew what I needed to know.

She was gone when I looked up,
but her perfume still lingered.
Sweet fragrance of hope.

TOMORROW

Spring debuts with shivers
and ends with a gasp
a giving in
a surrender to sweat
and sixteen hour days

it's then while listening
for sounds of change
a need for one more chance
a cool beginning

I think I hear a lullaby
a tender croon
hushing a howling world
with just one word

LIFE LIVED

When someone asks me
if I would do it again,
I say which part?
Which day?
Which hour?
Which minute?
And I do not know,
because we only know
after it is over.
When it is too late
to say yes or no
or even maybe.

Life lived
is an arrow
out of the quiver.
Shot from the bow.
Unable to be refired.
No practice makes perfect.
No practice.
No perfect.

Eve **Forti**, born in Boston, now lives on the coast of Maine with her husband, Tom. She taught elementary and high school and was a hospital chaplain, a campus minister, and a member of Spiritual Directors International for twenty years. She was on the Maine team that competed at the National Slam Poetry Finals in Asheville, North Carolina in 1994. Her poems have appeared in *Asheville Poetry Review, Atlanta Review, Off the Coast,* and *Common Ground Review* among other publications. She received six International Awards from *Atlanta Review* between 2007 and 2015. Her poem "Beautiful" won first prize in the 2013 *Common Ground Review* poetry contest. Her poem "At The Metropolitan Museum Of Art" was selected to be in the 2016 anthology, *Take Heart, More Poems From Maine.* It first appeared in her chapbook, *Holding My Breath*, published by Finishing Line Press in 2012. Finishing Line Press also published her chapbook, *Beautiful ,*in 2017.

www.ingramcontent.com/pod-product-compliance
Lightning Source LLC
LaVergne TN
LVHW041517070426
835507LV00012B/1639